Laughing
with My Hair Up

Hannah Pearl

Printed in the United States of America
First Printing, 2021
ISBN 978-1-949321-22-7

All writings within this book belong to the author.
Cover Art Image by: @kbearwrites
Cover Design by: Hannah Pearl
Illustrations by: @kbearwrites

A.B.Baird Publishing
66548 Highway 203
La Grande OR, 97850
USA
www.abbairdpublishing.com

Acknowledgements:

To my mama who means everything to me: thank you for your patience, selflessness, and encouragement. I love you the most.

To the family and friends that have supported me: thank you for cheering me on through days when I felt cheerless: I am forever grateful for you.

To Austie: when my mind grows weary, I will always remember the moment I read your message three times in disbelief. Thank you for believing in my poetry and helping me create the best environment for my book baby (your niece).

To KB: Thank you for the illustrations! They are beautiful and brilliant! I will never forget your kind eagerness to help out a fellow poet.

Table of Contents

The Mourning

Fallen from Grace	p. 10
Laughing with My Hair Up	p. 11
The Depression is Back	p. 12
Trauma I	p. 13
Golden Oldies	p. 14
Box Car Bargain	p. 15
I Have This Struggle With...	p. 16
Invisibly Broken	p. 17
Trauma II	p. 18
Isolation Dressed in White	p. 19
Recurring Dream	p. 20
Diseased	p. 21
Flare-ups	p. 22
Trauma III	p. 23
Let's Dive In	p. 25-26
Find Me a Waterfall	p. 27
Paralysis Agitans	p. 28-30
Daddy	p. 31
Burning Blaze	p. 32
Stained Wood	p. 33
The Saddest Love Story Never Told	p. 34
Good Luck Chuck	p. 35
Tied The Knot	p. 36-37
Intro/Outro	p. 38
The Lonely Nonet	p. 39
The Early Days	p. 40
Sleepless Roads	p. 41
Housekeeper	p. 42

Seeking Adventure   p. 43

Hindsight Is 20/20   p. 44

Halloween   p. 45

Seasons of Grief   p. 46

29   p. 47

Spirit   p. 48

Tiger Stripes in the Heights   p. 49

Photos Never Lie   p. 50-51

Fingerprints   p. 52

Stranded   p. 53

Stars   p. 54

Grieving in Dreams   p. 55

Pretty, Pretty, Princess   p. 56

Crackers and Crowns   p. 57

Fading   p. 58

"You Were There"   p. 59

Kate's Famous   p. 60-61

Poppet   p. 62

Future Promises to a Dead Girl   p. 63

E.E. Cummings Wrote it First   p. 64

Reflecting

Peeled   p. 66

Can't Be Tamed   p. 67

Practically Magic   p. 68

Will You Still Sing My Songs   p. 69

Caution!   p. 70

Compassionate Carly   p. 71

Without A Noise   p. 72

Therapy   p. 73

Wild Thing   p. 74

Don't call Me Beautiful   p. 75

The Places Our Love Remains	p. 76
The Art of Being Comfortable	p. 77
Hook	p. 78
Thirst	p. 79
Thursday Afternoons	p. 80-81
Moments	p. 82
Mirrored Memories	p. 83
California	p. 84
The Weight of the Waiting	p. 85
When Taylor Swift Sings, I Listen	p. 86
Memorials Make You Think	p. 87
The Desire For More	p. 88
Can you Find the Vein?	p. 89
I'd Never	p. 90
"Do You Wanna Hear A Joke"	p. 91
Policing Politics	p. 92
A Body Is A Body	p. 93
Privilege	p. 94
Sink or Swim	p. 95
Kiss Me	p. 96
Joker's Bluff	p. 97
Ambivalence	p. 98
Love Cuts Deep	p. 99
Lillies and Lavender	p. 100
Yearning	p. 101
Isabella	p. 102
The Morning	
Rest Here a While (Please Stay)	p. 104
Affirmation	p. 105
Save Me	p. 106
Full Circle Solstice	p. 107

Flirtations   p. 108

Forbidden Fruit   p. 109

Blossoming   p. 110

Echinacea   p. 111

Nitty-Gritty   p. 112

Purpose   p. 113

Lonesome, But Never Lonely   p. 114

A Worthy Choice   p. 115

Saturday Nights   p. 116

It Has to be Love   p. 117

The Way of Travel   p. 118

Victoria   p. 119

Shine On   p. 120

Flicker   p. 121

Something Like a Painting   p. 122

September 28th   p. 123

Early Sunday Mornings   p. 124

Here's the Truth   p. 125

Clocks   p. 126-127

Affirmation #2   p. 128

Raw   p. 129

Lay it on the Line   p. 130

About the Author   **p. 131**

The Mourning

Fallen from Grace

Somewhere along the way,
I stopped looking for the leaves
blowing in the wind.
They once hovered over me,
bright green and glowing.

And I don't
notice the sky,
its blue bellowing
beneath wisps of clouds.

When it's 64° and sunny,
I don't breathe in the air
like I used to.

I sleep with
the blinds closed.

Somewhere
along the way
my heart fell,

it scattered like
glass when it breaks-
loud and everywhere.

Laughing With My Hair Up

He pulls my hair out of its ponytail
and says this is what it
looked like when we met.
He says this is the way he likes it;
long and flowing, slightly disheveled.

I had forgotten
all, but the rosy cheeks
because I still get them
and they remind me of you.

It's not my proudest year.
I don't write much,
I carry more weight,
and I keep my hair up
because it's convenient
and I'm sad.

The Depression Is Back

There were
dishes in the sink
that she didn't
care to wash.
Dishes in the sink
for she didn't care
if she was caught.

Quite an accurate portrayal
of a person who forgot
that dishes left in the sink
meant she was much too weak
and much too soft.

Trauma I

My mouth tries to speak,
but my vocal cords are rusty
and they're flavored
with the taste of selenium.

My lips are pursed, but cracked
and when I lick them it feels
like deep river valleys.

Oh, but my jaw is the reigning queen-
every word left unspoken, she has
taken hostage with planned execution.
She holds tightly to the secrets my
body has yet to release.

Golden Oldies

Your voice haunts me.
The songs you sung are
mighty kitchen shears that

s / l / i / c / e

the veins
beneath the skin..
and will continue to
long after you're gone.

Box Car Bargain

When I tell you I'm
tired of being nice,
I'm actually exhausted.

This isn't a
little problem,
no, this is a
multitude of hands
to the forehead,
arms crossed over,
deep rooted sighs,
long drawn baths
with peppermint oil,
a messy tangle of
shampooed hair
with tears forming.

Foaming.

Lathering.

Rinse and repeat.

I know there's more to this life
than just being nice.
I feel it, like a rumbling purge
in the pit of my stomach,
like a freight train
headed toward collision...

until BAM

there's nothing left of me,

but ashes.

I Have This Struggle With...

...brushing my teeth.
Mundane task that it is,
but there you have it.

Get up.
Brush teeth.
Because as soon as
it's accomplished,
I can zip up the smile
just like yesterday's
pair of jeans.
May be a bit worn,
but I dress it in
grace and feigned esteem.

And there is a hole in the
tube of toothpaste
which I've grown so
accustomed to..

I don't fix it,
I just keep squeezing the
paste out the wrong way.

Invisibly Broken

I tell her
that my
silent cries
leave me
breathless and veiny.
She despondently
calls me a liar.

Trauma II

My jaw remains locked so that the
strikes from your words won't form
a pattern of bruises across my tongue.

Isolation Dressed in White

I'm afraid that this winter will be
the worst my mind has known.
That there will be too many
ugly memories to tackle at once,
too many negative voices to concentrate,
too much loss to consider.

I worry that this body will find too many flaws,
that these feet will get too lazy,
that these hands will never feel soft again.

I fear that my energy will fade,
my soul be weary,
and this heart,
well, I fear this heart simply
cannot be bothered to take
on anymore sorrow.

Recurring Dream

I tell my therapist
that it feels like I'm drowning.
The bubbles blown out from
deep synthetic breaths
right in front of me
and all I can offer is
a muffled scream.
It makes me choke.

I tell her no one can hear me.
No one sees my tears.
No one knows they
need to reach out
and grab my hand.

She asks me if that's the point in
the dream where I wake up.

I tell her, I'll let her know.

Diseased

My anxiety sets
tiny alarms off
in my brain if I
forget about it
for too long.

Fucking little monster.

Flare-ups

Why couldn't warm
summer days be filled
with cold lemonade
instead of harsh glares?

Whimpering winter skies
instead of hushed screams?

Though there was sweet spring
that never stayed sweet much.

And then in the fall; when the leaves
fade out and scatter before their death,
but the colors before it fly so bright with rage.

Trauma III

I know it's there.
I can almost taste the salt
I placed on the wounds
where you lashed out;
your tongue the most
evil part of you.

It's the sound of a slammed door,
the writhing beneath the
casualties of words
spilling out so easily.
It's not so poetic, but it's poetry.

Let's Dive in

It's usually the guess
that gets me.
I know I shouldn't
feel offended, but I do
because that woman,
she's my glue
and she'd never hurt me..
other than that time
where she let me go
too soon and I fell
flat on my ass.
CPS was called,
a cigarette burn,
one thought.
Two minutes in
that house with
her and they were gone.
No, not that woman.
She's my life's blood.

Then, oh, it must be him.
What did he do to you?
Now listen. I've got
plenty of daddy issues,
but absolutely none
have to do with abuse.
You'd have to be present.
Know my name.
Know my gender.
You'd know that my
humor comes from you,
because it sure as hell doesn't
come from the other side.
And I say sorry about
that comment like it's
going out of style,
but at least I'm honest.

Now that you ask,
yes, there was a boy once.
He was the age of a man,
but men don't hurt you like that.
They're boys that never learned lessons,
never learned not to treat a girl or a woman
like they were worn out hand me downs.
And those memories,
they're burned in forever.
Those lies perpetuated,
they've never been severed
because someone once told me
the same words before.

Why is it I look for
a repeated unnecessary
kind of love when I watch
films that tell me
it could be better?

Don't answer that.

You see, my abuser was an abusee
whether she'll admit it or not.
My abuser has a brain
of Quaker oatmeal
where there was once steel cut-
and I've been mad even so,
but for her it's not real-
It never has been.

See, she was sick long
before this sickness
and god, with her as my witness,
she never remembered one word.

She told me I was the crazy one.
Sound like a story you've heard?

See, I'm rhyming now because
these words fall off so easily,
like turkey off the bone with
Thanksgivings now turned grievous
because it hurts to go back there
as the only one who's aware.

Maybe one day I'll look to the skies
not only with the open-mind I'm so
praised for, but with forgiveness.

Find Me a Waterfall

I'm tired of swimming upstream.
I just want someone to tell me
it's okay to drift alongside the current.

Paralysis Agitans

Elle and I used to sing in her
kitchen to 90s tunes
while her mother and father
looked on with an
unfamiliar gleam
in their eyes.
They shared
winks and smiles
wide as the Tasman Sea.

We were eight
and still innocent as I
untangled the strings leading
me to the realization that a
traditional family was
the American dream.

I had just turned twelve in
the summer of '99,
when cancer took all,
but my mother's strength.
I watched as curls
fell to the floor
while we masked tears
with grim faces.
The stylist pruning a
shapely mohawk
working twice as hard,
solely to substitute our stoic
heaviness with laughter.

We celebrated good news
at the five-year mark,
when it's appropriate
to tell strangers that
you're a survivor.
This was the same year

I started to write
repetitious rhymes asking
where you were
and craving clues
on how you could
leave us in the
middle of such madness.

At twenty-eight,
I received a letter from
meddlers who never meddled,
relaying messages of mortality-
abandoning pieces of the puzzle
for me to unearth.

Paralysis Agitans.
Parkinson's.
A disease that
slows movement,
even though you
were constantly
on the run.

In a smoky cloud
of curiosity,
I wonder what
it was like
when you were no
longer able to
spring and
sprint gracefully,
similar to the horses
you once bet upon.

Here is where I decide-

that to think of
you shaking
doesn't shake me.
It's a death sentence

for a life I've
always lived without.

You are forever
in my thoughts
as the shadow of a man
who could've loved me first.

Daddy

I wanted there to be
a one day,
a someday,
or even just a thought
in your mind
that traveled
to me through
a letter,
or sign,
or pure
metaphysical affect.

I longed for a proudness to
resonate within you,
bringing out butterflies
from inside your belly
so that you would cry
out in awe.

I wanted for you to
read my words,
or see my face
in the distance
and grasp the reality
of a life unknown.

I wonder where you are now.
Surely, too dull to shine
identical to the stars in the sky.

Maybe you can find mercy
in the thick of the clouds,
but I imagine you'd still find a way
to fall right through them.

Burning Blaze

All the men in my life are devils.
The good ones won't touch me
with a ten-foot pole.
They can smell affection
that wreaks of desperation.
They breathe it in like air.
and spit it out like rancid milk.

Stained Wood

How did all
of my dreams
disappear into
the bottom
of a barrel
signed "survival"
in permanent marker?

The Saddest Love Story Never Told

I called you, "buddy"
because I was too scared
to admit I was falling.
You replied, "pal" with
the slightest bite
that I was almost positive
you had fallen, too.

And yet, after those
words were thrown,
The spell was cast,
and the only place
we fell was 'apart'.

Good Luck Chuck

I'm Good Luck Chuck.

Fuck.

Sorry if you
don't remember him.

He's the guy in that
film who just can't win.

Forget the
semantics
of it all
and the fact
that it's a
surly comedy.
There hasn't been
a better way to
describe this,
well, curiosity.

My main point is,
these men only want me
until they find a
better-looking fling.

I'm the thrown out
Cabbage Patch Carly,
replaced by Malibu Barbie.

And in the end,
she always gets the ring.

Tied The Knot

My brain shifted from
thoughts of you to the
angry pellets ricocheting
off the mess of dirty hair
I had clipped up in a claw.

Why were these flakes
so ruthless today?
Could it be we were
in the middle of a freak storm
that shouldn't be happening
for another two months?

Sure, it probably had something
to do with that whole
global warming thing.
Al Gore sure talked
about it enough.

I thought about how I
was doing my part
to help the environment.
I recycled.
I didn't sit with
my car on idle (most days.)
I turn the water off for
the two minutes
I brush my teeth and
I make sure my showers
don't last too long.

I suppose I could
have volunteered
to help pick up waste
or plant some trees
in my spare time.
I'd really get my
wings then, right?

But it seemed like
more than that.
Was it because we'd been graced
with a beautiful summer?
Maybe the fact that our fall was
the best one I've seen?
Full of blue skies
and short of rain.

Or perhaps it was that snow
was on my side today with
this whole "I do" exchange
happening over at the
Hyatt at 2 pm.

I checked my phone.
It was 2:38.

Intro/Outro

I guess I was just
some emotional fetish.
Someone that gave
you less stress.
Someone your eyes
didn't need to undress.
Someone that took you
from one level to the next.

I guess I was just
some foolish joke?
You blew me off,
I blew up in smoke.
Or perhaps it was
that you "misspoke"?

Yes, I'm sure that
was all that occurred.
I'm sure you never
 actually meant to flirt.
Never meant to end up
treating me like
backyard dirt.

The kind your dog shits in.
The kind in between your teeth
as your mouth grins.
The kind my
car wheels spin.

But don't worry
about me.
I've already
driven out of sight.

The Lonely Nonet

A bud called "love" sprouted in August.
Grew steady only to be picked-
rose petals scattered in the air
as its stem tore away.
The days grew shorter
and fall grew cold.
Wilted earth.
Dirty
death.

The Early Days

"You don't have to do
that you know", he says.

"Do what?" I ask.

"Hide your smile away."

I suppose hiding had
always been a necessity-
learned from years of
walking on eggshells.

I remember he told me
he'd relish seeing my dimple
as often as possible.

But those were
the early days

and dimples fade
when your heart
becomes a bruised
and battered wound.

Sleepless Roads

I fastened
your seatbelt
before you
drove us off,
but all you
gave me was
the third degree
and a bit
of whiplash.

Housekeeper

The lies spilled
out of your
mouth as easily
as a children's song
sung off key.

I've been picking
up these notes
and crescendos
around the house for days,
but the floor never stays clean.

Seeking Adventure

I've lived a whole day
while you were asleep
and I find it funny you think
I'd tire so easily,
but I feel wide awake
and ready for the
adventures you'll
never take me on.

I wasn't meant to
have days alone,
and I sure wasn't
made for settling.

I crave brightness and magic-
strong coffee and a lover,

longing, or aching, really,
for a soul to spend the mornings with.

Hindsight is 20/20

If only I had
seen it coming.
If only these
thoughts of mine
had a point to them.

Or a period on
the end of
a long, drawn-out
sentence to mark an
official goodbye;
like the one you so
casually slipped me
on that windy day in April.

Halloween

I always
looked at fall
through naive eyes.
But it's death.
Swimming
and dancing
around us.
It took me
till now
to see it.

And at 2pm on
Hallows Eve,
came the worst
brunt of all;
a cold front.

Seasons of Grief

It's in the colors you
don't see on the trees come fall,
or spring's stormy outbursts
fielding fits of rage.
It's in the dead of winter,
when snow is frozen and scattered.
Or in the hazy days of summer
when you won't hear
children's laughter
or maybe you will,
and you'll curse them.

On curtain drawn days you'll hear
the clock ticking in the silence
as you sip your coffee-
cold, burnt, and bitter
still feeling groggy.

People always say grief
comes in waves because
there are just too many
forms to name,
but I'm here to
tell you it's
multi-faceted
and maddening.

29

Suppose you had gone
the way of Plath;
just a year shy.
A grief unreasonable
to bear, yet you'll look
down the barrel
of what life you've yet to live;
solely to collapse,
or crumble,
or cave—
surprising in its ease,
to steal the breath
from your own chest.

In far too enormous a
concept to consider
or for the sake of
navigating the
mind around;
this faceless face is
merely a response,
designed to idly
haunt my waking hours.

Though at night,
you are whole again;
coming to me in dreams.
The unruly hair before you cut it,
the shelled necklace
before you outgrew it.
Your smile
(most misleading of all).
I forgive you.
I forgive you.
I forgive you,
even if there is
nothing left to-

Spirit

The final few leaves
hold on for dear life
at the first
falling of snow-
is that how tightly
you held on, too?

With mighty perseverance;
all the while knowing
that in the end,
the season always changes.
The leaves always die.

But then they do live again.
Their veins uncoil and
spring restores shades of green.

Maybe you live again, too.
Maybe today you're the sun.
Tomorrow, a wolf...
maybe next year, something else.

Tiger Stripes In The Heights

(Dedicated to all of the Heights Tigers.)

We lose a stripe annually.
Sometimes two...
and at worst, three.

These stripes hold no permanence.
They're not individual fingerprints,
sewn to tigers in the wild.
They fade slowly,
and tirelessly,
and they are forever missed.

When us tigers are
stripped of our stripes,
we weep out in agony,
scream with teeth bared,
tangled spit hanging
from the roof
of our mouths.

It's a different kind of pain-
walking those halls
without our tiger stripes in tow.

Photos Never Lie

I could've sworn
you were innocent-
your hair; a rat's nest.

In your white, red,
and gray sweater,
you clucked about;
resurrecting
laughs for free.
Your humor hung
like an iridescent
bulb that night;
flickering on
and then off
when no one
was the wiser.

When it was time for cake,
we lined up in a neat little row,
but your sneaker nicked
the side of the chair
that made a loud screech
and when people turned around,
you froze, waiting for
 a salvaged stillness.

You slept next to me
on the floor,
covered in sweetbriar roses-
it hid the wound
upon your chest.

Sad, how I
only notice now-
your wrist stretched out,
bare on the floor.

I finally fell into a slumber,
under sheets
of Mickey Mouse;
dreaming of lambs and lilies.

Even now, I wonder
if you slept at all.

Fingerprints

It was today
that I realized
you're the
constant ticking
narrative of
stories set to
the 'pre' or 'post'
of your absence.
You're the fixed
short hand of the
clock that marks
the time I can
never keep track of.

Stranded

There are still
pieces of you;
scattered in the
month of December,
where tired eyes and
restless souls reside.
Placed between
the lines of songs
that speak of the stars.

Fragments of you show up
in the simplicity
of an isolated shopping cart-
in the middle of a park
in Southern Australia.
Maybe you're
finding forgiveness
and solitude
amongst the clouds.
Or maybe you're
just thinking.
Of me.
Of us.
Of spoiled secrets
taken to the grave.

Stars

On a quiet night
surrounded by noise,
I concentrate on the sound
of my own breathing--
just so I can
remember that I am.

All too often,
we take in oxygen
without realizing that
so many others cannot.

Forgotten in
the years passing-
a mere story
that's brought
up in the absence
of a fairy-tale
or a lullaby
sung before bed.
But who sings to you now?
Can you still hear
the songs I hum
or are you too far away?
A speck in
the starry night
of silence and sound.

Grieving in Dreams

There were pins
in my mouth.

I couldn't speak,
couldn't hold
on to you,
couldn't apologize
for all that
I'd done.
Or all that
I'd undone.

Couldn't save
you with
those pins
in my mouth.

They were
just too heavy
and I was
way too unhappy.

Pretty, Pretty Princess

I never asked
you point blank
and you never
bothered to clarify,
but I know that time
in your bathroom
when those firemen
carried you out
naked and wet
that it was no accident.

The water had filled
up in your lungs
long before you
tried to wash it down
with your mother's
antidepressants.
Years before rumors
of multiple boys
started scratching
at the surface,
clawing at my eyes
for me to notice.
Long before you
screamed his name
when he had
"done nothing to you".

God knows now that
repetitive saying
is my strongest regret.

Crackers and Crowns

Every now and again,
my mind wanders
toward places
I never thought
I'd return to..

like cooking
goldfish crackers
in the heat of
a dirty flashlight
and laughing at
your dad because
he thinks we're weird.

Or the one time we somehow
suckered your brother into playing
Pretty, Pretty Princess
and then felt defeated
when he won the crown
and all the beautiful jewels.

Every now and again,
I'll grab a bag of
crackers from the store.
I'll wear a crown on
my head for New Years.
I'll think of you fondly,
but only sometimes.

Fading

I was asked
a question
I couldn't
Remember
the answer to.

I couldn't
remember...

...and I have no
one left to ask.

No one left to
share you with.

"You Were There"

Remember when Friday nights consisted
of confectionary treats and underrated films?
We used to roll the credits to one in particular as we
danced like little sugar plums beneath our falsa blankets.

Remember when we used to
creep into your mom's room on Sunday mornings
so we could steal her bed and cool white comforter?
I swear if you're in heaven,
that's what you're lying on right now.
I can't imagine anything feeling better
than that against my skin.

Remember when the two of us would fight about where
to end up on New Years, only to be satisfied with
staying in and watching the ball drop?

One year we made it as far as making plans
on the old landline in the kitchen.
I sat on the counter as you pleaded with me
to say "yes" to that party. I gave in.
You raised a fist in victory and then set it down
as you realized the only party worth
having that night was our own.

I may not have every single memory stored,
but I remember the small moments
that ended up being bigger than we knew.

I suppose I'll carry them with me,
as I do the lyrics of the song from that film..

"..cause my heart still remembers when you were around."[1]

---

[1] You Were There [Recorded by K. Edmonds]. (1998). On Christmas with
Babyface [CD]. Bradon's Way Recording: Kenneth "Babyface" Edmonds.
(1998, October 27)

Kate's Famous

Shredded cheese,
corkscrew noodles,
and don't forget the secret ingredient.
How secret it could be when the recipe
was from a famous cookbook that your sister ripped off,
I don't know, but we named it after her anyway.

Combing over receipts on the kitchen counter
as though they were thick penned
vows on thin paper napkins
where each dollar added up to the years
we spent loving one another
in this bizarre and uncommon marriage.

When we cooked together,
we'd throw in a little compassion here,
a dash of understanding there, and of course,
the communication it took to take turns stirring the pot.

The thing is, as time passed, we forgot to savor it.
Over the years we became used to it-
taking it for granted-
thinking we'd always have it-
that it would forever be there.

Eventually each new pot would echo
the silence that we couldn't ignore.
Trips to the store were less frequent,
sometimes a solo journey.

Receipts weren't necessary,
we knew it all by heart.
The stirring became repetitive
and, worst of all, obsolete.

If only they knew how
much I've craved it,
how over the years
I've tried to recreate it,
savor every single taste of it,
but there was always
something special that
was unrecognizable and missing.
A secret ingredient forgotten.

How I cringe when remembering the
beginning of a slow death that takes things
like a home and turns it into an asset.

I wish I could tell them all of this
now that you're gone, but I lost them
long ago in the divorce
with no hopes of reconciliation.

Poppet

I felt a prick or two today
as I was telling stories about you.
If I had known how big of a bitch
you'd still be up there,
I would've taken the
voodoo doll before you left me...

...or at the very least snatched up
those pins as they came tumbling
from my mouth and
into your thieving hands.

Future Promises to a Dead Girl

Say we meet here twenty years from now.
You end up with silver in your hair.
My wrinkles catch your eye.
I've thought about it so many times;
erasing that email before sending it,
taking the drugs out of your hands,
and shaking your mother awake.
I should have held onto you so I could have been
the one to feel the squeeze that the doctor
deemed an involuntary muscle spasm, nothing more.

Or maybe you'd never be there at all.
Maybe we rewind further
and I guard you each night
like a watchdog,
growl and claw at the
hands that dare touch you,
teach and preach from the soapbox
of an eight-year-old prodigy
because I'd know what I know now,
and I'd know exactly how to convey it.

All these future promises
to a dead girl,
when life is just
full of abandoned
shopping carts and
wilted flowers.

E.E. Cummings Wrote it First

Just as the trees,
I stood tall and grounded
in the guilt I felt.
Engulfing tides reaching out
to seize moments of joy.
A sea echoing her cries against the
high falling rocks that bounced off
the branches and leaves of
where I was planted.

You were lost before I lost you.
You were gone before leaving the earth.
Your bones soaked into the mud,
stealing the breath from all who loved you.

And you were loved,
despite it all.
You were the poem that
a famous poet wrote-
whether you knew it or not.

I always
carried your heart,
and here is where
I let it go.

Reflecting

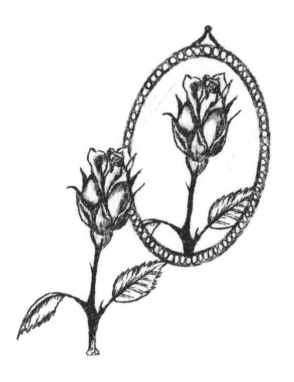

Peeled

In a family of swans,
I am the ugly duckling.
This is finally
realized at 22,
when all are grown
enough to sprout
up high, grow thick hair,
keep small waists.

I stand at 4'11
and sit on too many pounds.
But the mirror swirls its glass
back and forth,
making waves
to distort the image.

I sit back and sigh as she growls.
In her eyes, I sit on a pedestal.
I am the queen because
I am the only
one she knows.
I am only me.
Shouldn't that
be enough?

Can't Be Tamed

I know that somehow,
someway, in some
third dimensional world
that I am screaming.
I'm certain of it.

I can feel time standing still
and people frozen as I yell obscenities
and cry while spitting words
like nails at their faces.

I know it in my bones,
feel it in my face,
that I am fucking fierce
And reckless with abandonment.

And yet no one is
turning to stare
or crossing me with
their stern coal glares.

Who is this beast
I am imagining?
How can she be tamed?

Practically Magic

There is a slight rattling sound that
happens in the early hours of the morning.
It sticks to the walls like slugs
I know that's where it's home lies.

I tense up whenever I hear it.
I feel like it could be the end,
for a favorite film conceived the ticking beetle;
an unfortunate fortune for married men
who've fallen in love with the wrong witch.

I never think about the fact that
it could be announcing
a new beginning,
a fancier freedom,
a crack in the mundane,
an evolution of sorts.

Will You Still Sing My Songs?

Just like your
favorite musician
throughout the years,
my point of view shifts,
my eyes meet greater heights
forming mountain lodged slopes
that are made up of tiny regrets,
but bigger lessons.

My voice changes,
reflects differently,
molds smoothly to
a new moniker
and I am left
with the hope
that my words will
still touch you-
so far away,
yet so easy to
reach by mail.

Caution!

This vehicle stops
quite frequently
when overwhelmed.

It's me.
I'm the vehicle.

Compassionate Carly

It hurts you,
doesn't it?
Please tell me
it hurts you
like it hurts me.

That your stomach
ties in knots and
your dinners ruined.

That your eyes water.
That you say something
along the lines of
"I'm so sorry" in your head
before you turn back to
the conversation you were having.

Please tell me that
the sense of loss
isn't lost on you
when you see the
tufts of gray and
the white of bone.

This was a life.
A living and breathing life.
Calling it by name
is the least we
could do, right?

But we call it roadkill.

Without a Noise

I have this urge to write.
Because there's some
pathological demon
inside of me and
he won't quit.

Scribbling away is all
I can do to make sense of it.

It.
That.
This.

This "it" thing that
cannot be called by name.

But I'm here,
struggling to give up
an intangible wreckage.
I want anything that
makes me feel a little less alone,
even if it's clothed in sorrow.

I keep thinking
that it's obvious...
it's an obvious sign
that I am in need.

Still, no one calls.

And it's been years
since I've had a
hug that felt real.

Therapy

Thorns sit and marinate
in the thick of skin.
When they finally decided to,
they dispersed-
like tiny insects
scattering through veins;
navigating under the wound.

Silent as daybreak,
waiting for
a breath of change-

and with it,
belief.

And after it,
peace.

Spring brings
about buds
with rainfall to
help them grow.

Will the roses
ever know
their beauty?
And shall we?

For, we must be
able to bleed
atop a sharp spine
before we can
s p a r k l e.

Wild Thing

We are made of things.
Wild things.
Sullen things.

Wandering aimlessly,
we're a bountiful mess.

But, oh, it's beautiful thing to
weep among the fanciest willow tree.

A peaceful notion,
to run with the wind and not against it.

In the night, I feel threatened
by thoughts that all is temporary.

But oh, do I feel love in knowing it, too.

Don't Call Me Beautiful

I don't believe I'm beautiful.
Don't call me that.

Call me interesting or intense.
Fascinating or flawed.
Brilliant or belligerent
when intoxicated with anger.

Call me unwavering in loyalty
and sharp rather than smart.

Love me unconditionally
and without words.

Riddle me radiant underneath my skin,
encased within the ribcage.

Find the heart that's been
beating through all the mayhem.

But don't call me beautiful.
I won't believe you.

The Places Our Love Remains

Our love is still found
in the hushed lull
of my favorite song, or
between the ticking of the
seconds on a clock.

It's hidden in the blue jay's jeers
on a sleepy Sunday morning,
or the red-tailed hawks that they mock.

In a thousand different ways,
and without having to explain,
I discover moments when
I'm still allowed to quietly miss you.

The Art of Being Comfortable

Why are so many nights filled
with calls lost through the wires?
It's been lonely since I left,
but I fear you've been
lonely much longer.

And so then it would seem
that I was a breath of fresh air,
an opening in the skies,
if only to brighten your
cheeks with a rosy blush,
to send a sparkle to your eyes-
hungry for conversation and acceptance.

But now I am lonely me
and you are lonely you,
and we are separated by
miles of earth and deep oceans.

And yet all those calls are not lost-

they were simply never made.

Hook

As a child, I watched Peter
and the Lost Boys
as they tasted imaginary
corn on the cob
and guzzled down
invisible drinks
by candlelight.

But because they believed
with all their hearts
that the empty bowls
held the answer to life,
steam began to rise from
the tables as an endless
array of colorful pies appeared.

And if intangible fullness
or pure joy prove to be true,
I'd wake up in your arms,
covered in the sweetness
of a morning that never
knew of your absence.

Thirst

I'd given it enough time
or so I thought.

Time to recover from a
love unknown.
Unexplored.
Uninhabited.

So many "un"s
and never an "in".

Oh, to be invested,
infatuated,
or rather indecisive,

of how much I truly
could have loved you,

of the space in
my heart kept occupied
by the dull ache of muscle
that will never truly know peace.

Thursday Afternoons

We were young once;
dressed in overalls,
we played leap frog and
sold pink lemonade-
construction workers drinking
for only 10 cents a cup.

As teenagers we
fought over Jason Levy
in the back of the
same car where you
told him you loved him
without exchanging words.

And I looked back at the
brown carpet where you laid.
As you were,
and burned in my brain-
eating red grapes and
tracking sit ups.

Over in a corner
of a dim-lit room,
two young loves lay-
tossing M&Ms and giggling
like young loves do.
And only weeks later,
did they see the error of their ways.

Our "forevers" were made up in only
a myriad of hours,
soaking up the wine-stained tears
of the pseudo adults we claimed to be.

At 14 and at first sight, I fell in love
with Julian Mitchell just as
he was falling for
Olivia Lannigen
under the bleachers
during homecoming weekend.
I still don't remember
who won that game,
but it wasn't me.

Mike and I would speak
for hours on the phone,
counting our hits and misses.
We thought our world was small, then,
ignorant to how the swings we swung on
revealed the innocence we hadn't yet lost.

And here I lay,
echoes of names
in dreams slowly
stirred awake.

Here I am
and always will be,
forever dancing with
your ghosts.

Moments

Frayed sweaters, like cheap booze,
fade before their date's due.
Time is not sympathetic,
but to those few
that never turned their
nose up at a stranger.

It sinks into a heart,
like that of a couch being worn down,
or a favorite soft chair that's been
frequented by a sole occupant.

It's fragile, relishing in
moments moving too swiftly.
Current in the aroma of nostalgic
bonfires, in a tiny recall of your memory.

Captivating, but sad in that
it is comparable to
cracked skin, or bones,
that quiver under too much stress.

Swallowing your mother's words as you
remember her phrase it *just right*,
like an Irishman singing a lullaby;
"there she passes too quickly"

And that it does; time.
Ever the uncertain
in life's most certain
intangible matter.

Mirrored Memories

I told myself I'd stop loving you,
that I was moving forward,
wading through the heartbreak
swimming against the current like salmon
and as I was reciting these affirmations,
my voice faded away into the
memory of you and I at Vero Beach.
How we laughed and cried in the
midst of water sprays and seagulls dancing around us.
How we told secrets to each other.
How the sea pretended not to eavesdrop.

You found a snail's broken shell
and we gaped at it,
for it was strange to see it sliced right
down the middle like a lightning strike.
As if on cue, the sky rumbled
and the clouds came in.

I'm back in front of the mirror
and though I somehow stumbled
back to where I left off,
I don't even believe the half-naked
reflection starting back at me.
Not one bit.

California

Across an entire country,
I can hear the tears of children
in the thickness of clouds,
hazy with gray.

They're crying for their
tea cups and trucks,
their beds now burned.

I can hear the tears of mourners
in the glow of the burnt orange sun.
It bellows greatly in the echoes of
smoked wood and charred boots.

I see it sometimes;
the halves of houses still standing,
the eyes of animals barely breathing,
a flicked cigarette, a thrown match,
streaks of blue bursting...
into the land of the wildfires.

The Weight of The Waiting

I want to believe in heaven,
but I don't feel it in my bones
like some people.

Like a radical heat that flows
through them as angels get their wings-
what does that even mean... heaven?

A safe haven colored
in silver and gold,
a place that only stars
could dream about.

When Taylor Swift Sings, I Listen.

I felt heavy.
The kind of heavy that oversized
art books on coffee tables are made of.
My chest would plummet to my stomach
as I heard the last lines.

My heart feeling suffocated-
the kind of suffocation that comes from years
of solitude and hidden sanctuary.
My eyes, watering for the flowers sat upon
the kitchen counter, quickly losing their luster.

"She had a marvelous time ruining everything."[2]

And I,

I've never ruined a damn thing in my whole life.

[2] Dessner, A., & Swift, T. (2020). The last great american dynasty [Recorded by T. Swift]. On Folklore [CD]. Kitty Committee Studio, Long Pond, Sterling Studio: Aaron Dessner. Republic. (2020, July 24)

Memorials Make You Think

Whenever I go,
let them say whatever
they wish about me.

Call me weird,
riddle me insane,
consume my pages
so that you might even try
to make a guessing game out of my words
(I assure you, you'll be wrong.)

Let them tell others
they knew me well
and I'll be missed.
Let their tears be
genuine of a person
they regret they never knew.

But they cannot say I never gave
my whole heart to those I loved.

Or perhaps they could.

But I'd hear it and make sure
they trip over a rock later.

The Desire for More

Frightening is the epitaph
on my little block of land
that could read
for eternity:

Here lies Hannah.
She was nice.

Can You Find the Vein?

It's a child missing
or the stretch of silence
in a lover's goodbye.

It's a lick never played
or music unwritten

and I've seen
heartache in the eyes
of a person that hasn't forgiven.

It's a pair of brown eyes
in a lab coat
searching for a vein.
and I'm wincing.

Wrestling with fears.

Please find it here.
Please find it here.

I'd Never

The first time
I smoked a cigarette,
I coughed.
Not like the amateurs you see on film
that double over as they hack- no-
I coughed once,
and held the rest in.

I wanted a potent thrill to fill up my lungs,
needed the essence of this night
to be more than just what it was.

If I was going to die young,
might as well leave the earth
knocked off its orbit
with my brand-new bad habit.

"Do You Wanna Hear A Joke?"

I reflect on that time in the back of the van
when I first heard a punchline that
contained the word, n-gger.
It struck me.
Hard.
Like whiplash even though
we were at a stand-still.

It took me a decade to forget
then four more years to uncover
what had been forgotten.

Do I want to hear a joke?
Hmm..
Sure.

I couldn't tell you I
remember that one well either.

Something degrading about a woman's body
and how its primary function is to please a man.

I'm beginning to wonder if it's
called a *punch*line because I feel like throwing punches
or because I just roll with them.

Policing Politics

When a man loses his breath
at the hand of a blue-blooded criminal,
or a woman is shattered in her own home
by a name no longer biblical.

When a boy loses a game of cops and robbers.
When those with chocolate skin have been
beaten down and clobbered.

When will we listen?
What will spark the ignition?
When we will learn that love is not only loud,
but necessary by definition?

I house a rhythmic battle
between sadness and anger.
And I'm sorry to say that
"sorry" is no longer in favor.

To be quite honest, it never has been.

A Body is a Body

Whiteness has always reeked
from the stench of superiority.
But those with the darker tones,
those who have the same bones,
same heart strings- tug on them
and you know you're home...
because a body is a body is a body.

If you love how a
moonlit river glistens, surely you'd
love a Black girl's lips because
their skin is smooth as silk.
Beautiful like a black dahlia,
strong like a wolf pack alpha,
and they've never asked to be seen
as more than just human.
Give them the room then.

To breathe and live and be free-
to drive recklessly-
when the only things
taken away are keys
like when your rich
alabaster son speeds.
But I forget, that freedom
hasn't been what it seems.
Not for a Black girl
nor all the Black kings.

Privilege

You're afraid of saying
the wrong thing?
Say it anyway.
And be gracious in the
face of your ignorance.

For this culture of
mine will always be
ignorant to the fear
of losing a heartbeat to
the sound of sirens.

Sink or Swim

Why only write about the broken parts?
The parts of us that have nowhere to run,
nowhere to hide?
Other than the caverns of our hearts.

They build their residency in the shattered shadows
and when we feel those little monsters inside of us,
it's all we can do not to rip them out of our chest.

So we write.
We write them all away
until they come back to us again,
with their lawn chairs and beach hats,
riding the waves of all the tears we've swallowed.

But the beautiful parts? Those are sacred.
We keep those closest to us.
If they were to ever leave,
how would we survive?
How could we give those memories
permission to go if that's all
we have to hang onto?

And that is why our words
dive into the ugly places,
because we cannot stand the thought
of swimming out to sea
with our perfect memories in tow.
For what if they wash away with the current?

Kiss Me

What would it have been like?
Cautious and gentle?
Or with a passion intertwined
with years of searching?
I stayed up nights thinking of only this
and how beautiful it could be...

and how much respect
I would have lost for you
if you did.

Joker's Bluff

Love is not a game,
so the saying goes.
You'd think it would be
as easy as Trouble,
or strategic like Monopoly.
Perhaps it could be as lucky as Uno
or as anxiety inducing as Operation.

I'll tell ya, I have the best poker face
for a girl who's never mastered it,
but love's just not in the cards for me,
and I have never felt so much grief in losing.

Ambivalence

You can rarely tell if a heart
is ugly straight away.
You will save up too much
love for those people.
It will exhaust your
soul in the end.
Don't let it break you.

Love Cuts Deep

I received a gnarly papercut today.
You know how it slices you and
you don't feel anything until you see blood?

It got me thinking how bad the pain was.
To be cut by something so small,
so insignificant in the grand scheme of life,
but in the moment, you're aching for antiseptic.

I thought about my broken heart.
Thought about this evil boy
who did the damage of a man.

Thought about the fact that my life
was more pure before him
and more experienced after.
That what he gave me was
equivalent to a papercut.

He left me bleeding,
and with that came
antiseptic...
then band-aids...
and with that came new
skin forming underneath.

Lilies and Lavender

When there are days that
bring you to your knees and
you think you can't possibly take anymore,
look to the wildflowers.
They are as delicate as you and
they still withstand the wind and storms.
After the snow falls, they bloom...
again and again, without apology.

Yearning

On my
darkest days
I think,
God I would miss
this place after it rains.

Isabella

There is a longing to be awake-
to truly live-
to have just one iota
of the oxygen that
the redwood trees in
California bear and bestow.

One in particular; she grows,
in no means to alarm,
but to expand her breath;
as wise owls sat atop
her solid branches.
They challenge humanistic thoughts
with noisy questions
and gaze earnestly as
the sun rises and sets.

On hazy days when rain falls,
she stands tall and sees to it that the
wild honeysuckle receive the water
they so rightfully deserve.
Offering up their mouths in thirst,
she sprinkles droplets from her soaked leaves.

Over a span of endless blue skies,
she'll watch the river run dry,
knowing undoubtedly it will fill again.
Nothing is permanent.
Voids invariably fade,
as does our sadness.

I am the grass below her singing songs.
Whispering to the wind;
one day, I will not shake.

One day I will be as strong and
steady as the redwood.

The Morning

Rest Here A While (Please Stay)

I could get drunk off
the smell of fall;
and the dandelions that
wish themselves away
by the wind's angry mouth.

The bittersweet memories of bonfires
and a guitar's sweet melancholy
sweep me up in mid-October,
when the crisp air is at its peak.
And in a rainstorm,
I'll dance with
a binding faith.

Let this be the year you stay,
let this day be the moment
of infiniteness we have yearned for.
(I always ask this.)

But of course,
winter's blush comes through
in snowy skies and naked branches.

The dying leaves and I;
hushed in silent reverie,
we wait for time to stand still.

Affirmation

You are worthy
of feeling
incredibly and
unapologetically
a l i v e.

Save Me

The rocking chair
looked lonely
so I snuggled into it
and stayed there.
It was hours.
Maybe days.
I was lifeless.

I suppose I was only
sitting there to watch
the way the grass
grieves come fall,
as I do once winter nears.

Winter.
That cold soulless
son of a bitch that took
it all from me one year,
but then ended up saving
me in the end.

Full Circle Solstice

April is the month when leaves
take their first breath-
just babies in the cycle
that turns them
to dust come fall.

I live to take that
first breath with them.
Except I had been denied.
The very breath
within me refused to
exhale in late spring.

I've been holding it
in ever since.

'Let it go, let it go',
the trees swayed
while the leaves sang to me.
Under the palest gray skies of rain.

I cried as it washed me clean.

Flirtations

You had me at hello
is neither a statement
that fills me up or warms me.
It's a blush that bleeds through cheeks that
never knew trust.

Tell me something real;
something like a memory.
Something like a song your
ears know by heart.

Tell me she's only
there to fill the nights
that drip from the stains
of familiarity and affection.

Forbidden Fruit

If every feeling I could ever imagine
carrying in my achingly
tender and wandering heart
was put in a pot and brought to boil,
it would be last night's dream.

I swear I smelled the berries melting,
tasted the faintness of
bitters on my lips.
Sipped it slowly as I would a
frothy cream liquor
or a vodka martini.
And just like that-

one quick punch to the gut—
one flutter of an eyelid—
and it was all taken away in the shaken,
stirred awakening of daylight.

Blossoming

Your happiness may
look like freedom.

A good book.

An aged bottle of wine.

So take that plane ride.

Wrestle with the
emotions of characters
both good and bad.

Taste that bittersweet red
that leaves you dancing clumsily
in your midnight blue dress.

Be happy whenever
you have the chance.

Life is too short
for constant sorrow.

Echinacea
I am finally healing.
Not only by feeling,
but by sitting with it.

Not eating through it.
Not sabotaging relationships.
Not biting the insides of my cheeks
nor stuffing a metaphorical gag down
my throat to keep the hot ash tears at bay.

I am sitting with them;
these feelings.
Welcoming them.
Letting them rest a while
with a cup of tea.
They swirl their
Echinacea with teaspoons,
refusing sugar cubes and honey,
beckoning for more before they've even finished.

And then I don't will them away
like an unwanted guest,
I allow them to
leave as they came.

Harshly.
Swiftly.

And with consent.

Nitty-gritty

I'm not your average
creamy hazelnut latte
placed beside the
bedside table on a
lazy Sunday morning.

I'm an enlightened
dark roast with
vanilla notes.

I'm the reason
caffeinated patrons
tell their baristas
to give it "that jolt".

The kind you need
come Monday morning
before the weekend's fog has lifted.

Impossible to greedily sip...
just take it a little at a time,
pretend to be the humbled adult
by tightening your lips as
you choke me down
because you could never
handle me in my purest form.

Purpose

What happens in the
early hours of the morning
when you're stirring in your sleep
as you dream up ideas and tell them to
fuck off because you're too tired?

Only to awaken to the thought of
having missed out on an elevated,
enormously powerful, highly sought after
version of you.

Sleep is for the dead.
Remember that every time
you're beckoned to come alive.

Lonesome, but Never Lonely

I met him on a whim in late May.
We talk of issues and interests
close to our hearts.
We seem to slide off
one another,
like a slick bow on
a violin's strings,
perfectly in tune.

Tell me why, then,
do my thoughts lead
back to you
when the man
in the moon
frowns down
to me from his
black, silk sky on
a lonesome Saturday night?

A Worthy Choice

When I get
the chance to sleep
in a queen size bed,
I sleep in the middle.
I don't pick a side
nor do I want to,
but you've got
me thinking
maybe I should.

Saturday Nights

I wonder if you realize the way
your fingers move, moves me.
The sounds of your guitar
weaving together and
traveling through
it's carved wooden base.

I wonder if you're aware
that every time you open your mouth,
I want to sing the notes with you.
To drift into a dreamy haze
where fairytales are spoken in
rhythmic melodies on the tips
of our tongues.

It Has to be Love

I want to drink you in,
like bittersweet red,
or spiced hot cocoa,
I want to eat the words of your praise
and taste every little morsel.

The Way of Travel

I always figured
that true love
would find me
in my own backyard,
but perhaps I
had to follow it;
flying past
buildings and seas
all the way to
a foreign land
that made me
feel alive.

Once.

Victoria

I found a compass in Cleveland, Ohio.
It pointed south and so I went--

further

   and

      f u r t h e r

until I reached the foreign soil
that felt right under my bare feet.

I held out that same compass,
but it did not point.

It had no arrows left.

It read;

south.
west.
east.
north.

she'll
wander
earth,
nevermore.

Shine On

We don't often think
about how the sun sets on
different objects and places
during all hours of our day.

How there may be shadows
where there was once illumination.

How it can change
in 1/8 of a second.

How the light will
shine on you again...

and trust me, it will.

Flicker

I'm trying to
light all these fires
in the absence of sun.

Something Like a Painting

I'm going to take these tears
and turn them into works of art.

Watch them cascade
over mountains,
be enveloped by wind,
run the valleys ragged,
soar over clouds and rooftops,
landing in underdeveloped gardens
that I will soon turn lush and green.
So green that the birds flying above
will be envious that I could create
such beauty from this pain.

So green that my heart will forget
ever loving you in the first place.

September 28th

I've carved out colors
in the absence
of a detailed memory-
a sketch of fragments
to remember for
years to come;
a single photograph
with trapped glances in time.

The night you first
held me without inhibition,
your whispered flirtations
dancing upon warm breath
and your hushed promises,
that were never to be brought up again.

These things didn't matter so
we chased our delusions as fast as
we chased the fireflies over that hill,
and all we wanted was to enjoy
the moments we were given.

Because you
were only borrowed;
and I was a mere dreamer.

Early Sunday Mornings

We rehearse retired movie lines;

It's this tango that we do-

                    slow,

quick, quick,

          slow.

Happens only for
the briefest of moments,
yet I've grown accustomed to the beat-
mostly because it feels a little like home.

Here's the Truth

There's a person
at the other end
of the world
that sits across
from you at the
dinner table every night.

I'd will it to be me
if I could.

Clocks

Time keeps
slipping through
fingers once
intertwined
by yours.

Ticking...

Ticking...

Ticking...

as if it's to say...

you are running out,
running scared,
or standing too still.

Some days it
harbors a sound so loud
that I expect my breath
to catch in my throat-
that it will swallow me whole.

Sometimes I go out
in the evenings.

Sometimes I don't.

But you.

You are just a thought away.

A flash of orange
in the corner of

a local pub,
a lyric in an
eighties song overhead.

It always brings
me back to you.

I glance at the
clock and wonder...

what you're doing
at this exact moment...

...who you are doing it with.

If you ever stop when
both hands hit 11 to think of me.

Affirmation #2

Just in case anyone
failed to tell you,
your struggles are
just as important
as your accomplishments.

You aren't
one whole mood,
you are several.

And that
is beautiful.

And that
is the journey
of a human being.

Raw

I used to care what people
thought of my words.
Would they hold
too much honey?
Would they be
crude or crass?

God, how ashamed I'd feel
to utter a description
of a person covered
in my own convictions.

Then something
magical happened...

A sort of
"burning blaze"
bubbling toward
the surface.

And I was
a cured poet-
now a woman
of my words;
proud and bold
and beautiful
in my statements.

How lovely that
I am finally fitting into
clothes suited for a writer.

Lay it on the Line

Most of me is
too scared to
move forward;
for others to
know my insides
and pick apart
my words
which they can
only try to comprehend.

Maybe it can
resurrect feelings that
they've long buried
because I've said
something
that struck a nerve...

and if you
are reading this,
in between pillow soaked tears
and beer brewed evenings,
you'll see it-
the proof needed
in finding the
will to dream big.

Hannah Pearl is a 33 year old ABA tutor living in Cleveland, Ohio. She has worked in customer service, special education, and with children, yet her soul passion has been to become a published author. This passion was brought to fruition during a year of intense struggle, and also, inner peace.

Pearl is no stranger to struggle. She has been down the parallel roads of both anxiety and depression. Though she has traveled far and wide to visit some truly remarkable corners of the world, Pearl has had many a setback; the toughest of journeys taking place inside of her own mind. True to her namesake, Pearl has developed those grainy trials and tribulations into things of beauty.

Laughing with My Hair Up is Pearl's debut poetry collection and as such, she has taken up space within these pages to provide the audience with plenty of heartbreak, trauma, introspection, and turbulent life lessons.

In the midst of a pandemic, Pearl became acquainted with Instagram and has made a name for herself within the poetry community. She posts about love, heartache, grief, and mental health.

To discover more of her writing, Hannah invites each of you to join her Instagram family at @earthypearlpoet

Made in the USA
Monee, IL
01 May 2021

67441851R00080